The Narrow Gate

Robert Stewart

The Narrow Gate
Writing, Art & Values

Robert Stewart

* * *

There is no "must" in art, because art is free.
   — Wassily Kandinsky

The Narrow Gate: Writing, Art & Values

Copyright © 2014 Robert Stewart
All rights reserved.

No part of this book may be used or reproduced in any manner whatsoever without the prior written permission of the copyright holder except for brief quotations in critical articles or reviews.

ISBN: 978-0-9913281-5-4

Cover art: "Sash 2013," tape, monoprint, collage on tape, by Garry Noland. Photo by E. G. Schempf

Serving House Books logo by Barry Lereng Wilmont

Published by Serving House Books
Copenhagen, Denmark and Florham Park, NJ
www.servinghousebooks.com

Member of The Independent Book Publishers Association

First Serving House Books Edition 2014

The author thanks the artists and poets who allowed their work to appear here with these essays: Garry Noland for his cover art, "Sash 2013," and the photo of his "Bench 1"; Gloria Baker Feinstein for her photograph "Waterfront Park 4, Portland, Ore."; Mia Leonin for her poem "Nurse's Epitaph"; Ellen Pearce for her painting "Holy Land"; Allison Eir Jenks for her poem "The Lord Is Easy to Please"; Roi J. Tamkin for his photograph "Red-Winged Blackbirds"; Mary Crockett Hill for her poem "Woodbridge"; Lisa Grossman for her painting "Flatwater II"; Wendy Barker for her poem "I'm Not Sure the Cherry Is the 'Loveliest of Trees'"; Marilyn Kallet for her poem "To My Poem of Hope." Copyright for their work remains with them.

for Robert Balice Stewart
for Lisa

Contents

Introduction / 9
Heroes / 11
Resilience / 15
The Narrow Gate / 21
On Wishful Thinking / 24
Typhoon / 30
Glory / 32
Form / 34
"All That I Remember" / 36
Art + Work / 40
Fast and Slow / 45
Service / 47
Time and the Fabric of Immensity / 49
Literary Values / 53
Take This Seriously / 57
Power / 61
Madness / 67
Cry of the Renegade / 71
The Goldilocks Zone / 74
Faith / 77
Notes / 80
List of Poems Included / 80
Acknowledgments / 81
About the Author / 82

Introduction:
An Editor Attempts the Impossible

Art is not vague production, transitory and isolated, but a power that must be directed to the improvement and refinement of the human soul.
— Wassily Kandinsky

I like little books and have tried to achieve, with this collection of essays, the paradoxical virtue of great little books I have known — such as *Night Flight*, a novel by Antoine de Saint-Exupéry, or *Wind, Sand and Stars*, essays by Saint-Exupéry, or *In Praise of Shadows*, by Jun'ichirō Tanazaki, or *Concerning the Spiritual in Art*, by Wassily Kandinsky. Tanazaki says that Japanese music is above all a music of reticence, so it is this book attempts its own brand of restraint. Not too much. Not too loud. It actually surpasses most of those other books in virtue of being small, but this smallness attempts a larger good; I wrote each essay to be condensed and contained, to compress as much feeling for art as I could into the smallest, workable form.

Each essay originated as an introduction to writing and visual art contained in certain editions of *New Letters*, a magazine of writing and art from the University of Missouri-Kansas City. The magazine comes out only three or four times a year, but I nevertheless wrote each opening essay as close to the deadline as possible. I wanted urgency and directness; I wanted pressure to grind down the brush pile of my thoughts to fiber or pith, wherein something I had not known would emerge of the essential nature of literature and art. If I think about it, the task might be too big for editor or writer, but this is what I love.

"My aspiration is to create a kind of nongenre," poet Charles

Simic has said in *The Monster Loves His Labyrinth*, his own little book of prose — "made up of fiction, autobiography, the essay, poetry, and of course, the joke." That sounds impossible, I want to say, but in such things lie our aspirations.

I hope these essays retain for you their spontaneity. If you wonder what makes reading literature worth your time, or if you sometimes wonder why your own making of art matters, perhaps something of value will appear here with a degree of suddenness. Maybe an idea will be sharp-edged enough to open a cut somewhere.

— R. S.

Heroes

Giles Corey lived in Salem Village in the late 17th century, but what matters here is his ongoing life in Arthur Miller's play *The Crucible*. In 1692, Corey stood accused of having served bread and wine at a witch's sacrament; and, for legal and moral reasons, he refused to accept the charges or stand trial. Since my first reading of the play, in college, one moment has remained emblematic of what personal conviction looks like: When Corey faced the court, he simply refused to participate, to confess or console the prejudices that faced him. Great stones were laid on his chest, Miller writes, until Corey would agree to plead either aye or nay. "They say he give them but two words," reports a girl witness in the play: "More weight."

I would like to have met Giles Corey, but no more so than Arthur Miller, himself. On the occasion of Miller's death, Feb. 11, 2005, having missed my chance, I continued to believe that showing up in person to meet the masters, the great people, even briefly, uplifts us. Recently, I heard that a writer whose short stories I admire was doing an interview at a local radio station. I won't drop the name but will say this: When he stepped out of the studio, I was there. "I just want to shake your hand," I said. It occurs to me that I was alive when Hemingway was alive, but I was too young and witless to go shake his hand. The same goes for Picasso, Martha Gellhorn, Langston Hughes, Henry Miller. Each has presented moments in art that have shaped me and helped shape the world.

Arthur Miller would have been harder to meet than most, no matter how great, if only because his four-year marriage to Marilyn Monroe — herself alive when I was alive — gave him status more like a prince, or, in this land, a president. The question is, can a momentary encounter, a dinner, a drive to the airport, a drink, really amount to anything profound, as we might imagine a touch on the cheek by Christ, the Buddha, or, in our own time, a Wangari Maathai? Let's say it affects us to the degree the person's work affects us. Sitting at a dinner table with the poet of "The Amen Stone," Yehuda Amichai, for example, helped even me understand the startling fact that spiritual transcendence can come from us human beings.

I am told that in person heroes can be disappointing. The observation has become predictable, hackneyed, always cynical. Sure, they hit on our women, drink too much, or just want to be left alone. What goes unsaid is that such disappointments serve our spiritual purposes, as well. My own friend and mentor for many years, David Ray, has written of when he, as a young poet, approached the great Robert Frost to have a book signed. "I don't sign paperbacks," said Frost. That story gives me hope that any of us might overcome our own pretensions, as Frost surely did long enough to write "Stopping by Woods on a Snowy Evening."

I once arranged for the now Hall of Famer George Brett to record a 30-second radio "promo" for the radio program *New Letters on the Air*, and in preparation developed a grand dream for myself, that Brett and I would strike up a friendship, go fishing together, hang out. That was 1980, and Brett was hitting at the time over .400; bumper stickers proposed "George Brett for President" — though that November, Ronald Reagan took the crown. I found Brett in the Royals' locker room before a game, sitting back, reading a book. He had not been notified of our arrangement or of my dreams, and I barely convinced him to proceed with the recording. "Okay, let's go into the laundry room where it's quiet," he said. Then, quickly, albeit grudgingly, he began to read the script I had prepared: "This is George Brett. Whenever I or my teammates on the Kansas City Royals want to listen to great poetry, we tune in . . ." He read my odd, outrageously condescending script in one take, smoothly, without flinching, which I never have ceased to admire. I had thrown him a curve, and he went down and got it.

In the course of my job, I have had the honor of visiting at least briefly with the likes of Mona Van Duyn, Etheridge Knight, Gwendolyn Brooks, Donald Justice, Stanley Elkin, all of them — mostly gracious, at times testy or challenging — were sanctified by their humanity. Years after that earlier meeting, David Ray wrote a poem of thanks to Robert Frost that includes these lines: "Hope for the past, / yes, old Frost, your words provide that courage." Being in the presence of people such as Frost, or David Ray, himself, offers a connection to each person who has leapt what B. H. Fairchild describes in one poem as "the vast gap between talent and genius." Fairchild means, between the ordinary and the transcendent.

In any issue of *New Letters* or another magazine, perhaps, you will experience the work of just such writers, your neighbors, your friends, people who could jostle beside you on a subway or bus. We find people engaged in acts of courage, even heroism, taking what's laid on them and responding with the literary equivalent of Giles Corey's defiant "more weight," that is, with their new work.

"Waterfront Park 4, Portland, Ore.," photograph by Gloria Baker Feinstein

Resilience

One of my writer heroes, Jack Conroy, in his pre-*Grapes of Wrath* Depression novel, *The Disinherited*, has narrator Larry Donovan setting paving bricks in a road during a sun-blasted summer. "I was thirsty enough to spit cotton," Donovan says. Conroy, himself, survived a Depression winter by eating carrots he dug with a pick from a frozen field. We don't know yet how new weather extremes will affect us in the long term, but here in western Missouri, the summer of 2012 seems haunted by John Steinbeck's depiction of 1930s drought. "Now the wind grew strong and hard, and it worked at the rain crust in the corn fields," he writes. "Little by little the sky was darkened by the mixing dust." I have felt that dust in parts of eastern Kansas this summer, though not with a darkened sky as those days. My wife, Lisa, started out by horseback this May and rode, solo, four weeks and a day through Kansas and Missouri farm country, in heat that, in the early weeks of summer, reached 100 degrees only on a few days. At the start of her ride, farm ponds still looked full and the young corn green with promise.

By mid June, however, the heat and dust became hard to endure. Her horse, Chief, learned fast that he no longer could find a convenient trough in his comfy pasture, and he'd better drink up whenever he got a chance — usually water my wife carried from a pond in her collapsible bucket. Meanwhile, at our suburban home, the back yard evolved into a little dust bowl, loathe as I am to pour water onto grass. At least one stock-market analysis website has invoked *The Grapes of Wrath* to predict what might happen to our farmer friends in 2012 and beyond.

Literature and art almost always give people extreme circumstances — morally, psychologically, physically — to deal with. Art tests us and does not back down. I look at photographs by Gloria Baker Feinstein of kids playing in a fountain, yet I feel mostly the intense heat of summer around and outside the frame. "The relationships in art," Wassily Kandinsky has said, "are not necessarily ones of outward form but are founded on inner sympathy and meaning." In that distinction, between outward form and inner sympathy, I have found examples to sustain my capacity for hope.

Donald Hall in his memoir "A Yeti in the District" seems to have, in time, washed away any evidence of himself. "Visits to Washington have punctuated my life," he begins. After what he says was likely his last visit, a writer for *The Washington Post* made it her business to ridicule Hall's very appearance in a photo with President Obama. "My mouth is open in life's widest smile," Hall writes, "as I confront the neatly dressed Obama in my sports coat and khakis, with my frizzy hair and reckless beard. I thought," Hall continues, "it was the best photograph of my life." It surely was. His life in literature, seen through the culture of our nation's Capitol, tests the resilience of an artist in a culture of glibness. Hall seems to be putting his big, sweet, tender hands to our faces in comfort.

Let me offer two qualities found wrapped inside most great writing and art: love and gratitude. If literary art does not ultimately relieve us of hopelessness and cynicism, then I don't know why we bother. A researcher for the Harvard School of Public Health, Dr. Laura Kubzansky, reported in 2007 and again in 2011 on the healing effects of what she termed "emotional vitality." Resilience is the key, she said, to physical and mental well being. Literary readers generally know that some positive movement must come out of the process born by struggle, even tragedy. "Soft nurse of dear idea, near me stay," wrote 18th-century poet Ann Yearsley and quoted in "Nurse's Epitaph" by poet Mia Leonin. That quote implies nurture, engagement. Forgive me if logic and rationality bend a bit to hope and intuition, but if emotional vitality remains a goal for psychological and thus cardiovascular health, perhaps we can extend that to our engagement with each other and with nature, also.

My wife's, Lisa's, ride included more extreme challenges than I know; but I did learn a few things about rural life: There are a lot more family-owned, small farms and ranches than I formerly believed. Farm families answer to Amish, Mennonite, Lutheran, Catholic, Baptist, and everything else in the range of faith and nonfaith, and, as it turned out for my wife, all amounting to much the same sort of people — loving and grateful. She met older men who choked up with affection for their wives; she met kids who said, *Yes, Ma'am,* when spoken to and rode alongside her awhile when she said goodbye after a night on their land; she met women who rode, carried rifles, cooked, farmed and told good jokes. Like Jack Conroy, whom I knew in his later years, the people who live now, in the drought of 2012 in the rural Midwest, sustain us with their resilience.

I am not saying times are easy. Yet in a poem by Jo McDougall we hear an imagined Flannery O'Connor say from the grave, warning off all fretful souls, "Go away. And take / that maudlin moonlight with you." So she says, in "Standing Alone at Flannery O'Connor's Grave in April, a Woman Hears a Voice." McDougall's hero, in the voice of O'Connor, as with Conroy and Hall, asks us to look past the outward forms. "Don't give me that simpering look," she says.

Emotional vitality, research suggests, holds at least the possibility of a restorative biology; and the stories we tell each other have their own restorative qualities, I believe. Try this example: At the end of each day, without fail, Lisa would find some family of strangers, on some randomly chosen gravel road, that would always offer her horse a pasture for the night and her a place to pitch her tent. Often, they brought her food and coffee, invited her inside for a shower, posed with her for pictures in the morning, exchanged phone numbers and email addresses, and, more often than not, teared up when they said goodbye. Each day, every day.

NURSE'S EPITAPH

Mia Leonin

> *Soft nurse of dear Idea, near me stay.*
> --from "Absence," Ann Yearsley

She's a diabetic who craves strong sugary drinks –
a gaggle of maraschino cherries bobbing
to the surface of a tequila sunrise.

She once placed a small square transistor radio
in the crib of a thalidomide baby. Mongo Santamaría's congas

crackled on the moist pad and through the metal bars –
nose hole, eye pit, tuft of hair pulsed in perfect rhythm.

Kneeling among the orange vinyl bean bags, she poured
cans of vanilla Ensure into the stomach tubes of hydrocephalics –
frail bodies tethered to helium-blown skulls.

On the weekends, she brought home crippled toddlers and Down Syndrome
kids with names like Cowboy and Jodie.

She once saved a dog's life with the Heimlich maneuver.
The chicken bone shot across the room and dented a metal cabinet.

All those children and dogs are dead now.
My mother's slippers shuffle across the tiles of my house.

"Holy Land," painting by Ellen Pearce (*original in color*)

The Narrow Gate

"Holy Land," Ellen Pearce's painting on the cover of *New Letters*, draws viewers with its bright yellows and reds. "Beautiful," I often hear; then the viewer realizes, "Those are bombs. That's blood down there." If art demands transcendence, it does so through the visible, the actual, and allows us time to see beyond. Not for no reason does Pearce's painting include a non-natural opening of light, a rectangle, like a door or window, something human-made we might call an alternate choice. The artist, there, gives us a "narrow gate" to go through — as the gospel of Matthew advises in Willis Barnstone's *Restored New Testament* — among the wide-ranging and nearly organic images of war. I see the squared-off shape that way because I choose to, and because I can. The artist leaves the choice, finally, to me. Look at it.

Art seeks that magical brightness, which is not often easy, not often expedient. I write this on the Feast of All Saints, which would seem the height of convention, even comfort, among churchgoers. Not so. The saints won't let it happen. Take "saints" here in the larger, unofficial view — as Emerson wrote, "When the half-gods go, / The gods arrive." This morning, I heard a Jesuit priest celebrate an Austrian farmer by the name of Franz Jägerstätter, a husband with three daughters, and the only Roman Catholic in his town, in the early 1940s, to declare himself anti-Nazi. When Jägerstätter asked Church authorities to explain the contradiction between Church teaching and the Church's own acquiescence to Hitler's policies, they couldn't. They said what others in their position have said over the years: They were just following orders. Those orders formed the wide landscape of that time and place. In 1943, Jägerstätter refused service in Hitler's army and chose, instead, to go through the narrow gate — into prison, in his case, where the forces of the Third Reich cut off his head.

The story dramatizes something more important even than heroism. It alerts us to the ease with which we, as a culture, can come to accept the wide landscape as normal and acceptable. I often have wondered how I would have responded to certain historical events, and I have no confidence that I would have done the right or the brave thing. I am encouraged, however, by the fortitude of others, such as our interview subject in this issue, poet Edward Sanders, practicing his convictions on behalf of peace and nature, at the age of 70. I am inspired further by the Miami-based writer Mia Leonin, who asked if she could guest-edit a section of poetry in response to our present wars.

This has nothing to do with the validity of any particular religion, or of religion, itself. It concerns our ability to act out of conviction. All of these writers can be called fierce, even when facing internal dilemmas — like military vet Roy Scranton, pondering his left-over military gear: "I want to keep everything. I want to throw it all away." Such stories, poems, and essays have been built by people in various stages of doubt and trepidation; they are personal and political and cultural; and every one required conviction to write.

"To believe fully and at the same time to have doubts is not at all a contradiction," writes philosopher Rollo May in *The Courage to Create*. "It presupposes a greater respect for truth, an awareness that truth always goes beyond anything that can be said or done at any given moment." Rollo May understands the dual nature of art, especially literary art, in which a reader or character comes into conflict with a prevailing force, external or internal; and someone, reader or character, will be called to make a choice. What could be more exciting, or important?

Franz Jägerstätter has been beatified by the Church but not yet canonized. Here's the good news. He already has made his stand, which is what matters. And more good news. Ellen

Pearce does not say what she intended by that rectangle of light in her painting "Holy Land." Maybe she expects us to step through.

On Wishful Thinking

"*Life is a gift. Love is life*" observes a preacher's sign in a poem by Allison Eir Jenks, called "The Lord Is Easy to Please." The Jenks poem admirably resists pointing out that the sign is an example of wishful thinking, which doesn't make the sentiment untrue but merely empty of spiritual value. The paradox of poetry and fiction, of creativity itself, is its intellectual nakedness. If I, as editor, have done my job well, you, the reader, will be spared the disease of wishful thinking. The Chinese philosopher Mencius could have been reading such a sign when he wrote, "I hate glibness, for it will be mistaken for righteousness."

"In the morning," writes essayist Floyd Skloot in a memoir about his and his wife's trip to Paris, "my spider bite began to recede." The essay, "Travels in Lavender and Light," exposes a journey where almost everything goes wrong, until near the end he adds, "I was running out of maladies to write about." Skloot's ability to look at the Paris trip directly, for what it was, not for what he wished it were, is a small example of a great virtue — what poet John Keats described in a letter as the humble standard of disinterestedness. Skloot says of his and his wife's trip, "We might not miss it, we agreed, but we'd remember it." Disinterested writing goes fearlessly toward direct apprehension of the elements, presenting details to people whose assent will not automatically be given.

My early training as a poet came partly from a group of friends close to my age, mid 20s to early 30s, and many of them now, after years, have become successful playwrights, novelists, poets, computer technicians, lawyers, and entrepreneurs. Some are dead. We had a kind of fervor to us that demanded blunt, direct, often, in retrospect, embarrassing statements of what is. We read Muriel Rukeyser's "The Poem as Mask," and its injunction, "No more mythologies," which we took to mean, nothing that isn't true and anything that is. No censoring ourselves or anyone. Bodily functions, personal relationships, named names — all material for poems and discussions in front-porch workshops.

"When the mind knows its inner-most ideas will be exposed to nonprofessional outsiders," write Carol Bly and Cynthia Loveland, in a 2006 book called *Against Workshopping Manuscripts*, "the mind will screen back its keenest ideas in order to avoid contumely." Our group — among them, Higgins, Field, MacLean, Sandler, Wagner, Mbembe — while hardly professional, then, was of a mind: We cultivated directness. If I can say anything about us, we did not cultivate what Bly and Loveland describe as "fear of one's peers."

Ask Jenks' preacher to read Adrian C. Louis' poem "Note to a Pine Ridge Girl Who Can No Longer Read," about his wife, suffering from illness. Life might be a gift, but it also can be dirtied adult diapers, and the wife's two fingers that had to be cut off, and the speaker's confession, *God forgive me for okaying that*. We can dispense with the phrase "Love is life" because Louis' poem shows us what love actually looks like.

In "The Lord Is Easy to Please," Jenks places herself in the netherworld between the ideological purity of churchgoers and her speaker's alcoholic mother. The common appraisal tells us that poets must live in such an in-between place — outside both formal group prescriptions and self-absorption. Artists, themselves, might not always achieve that place, but the closer truth is this: That is where art, itself, must live.

William Stafford's great poem "On Being Called Simple by a Critic" lives in that netherworld, which is neither of self-justification nor of retribution for the critic's contumely. The poem appears to be about plums — "I wanted the plums, but I waited," it begins. Stafford thanks the critic for his or her honesty. The poet simplifies his life. He lets the plums be plums. He practices humility with a joke on himself — opening the fridge, he says, "Sure enough the light was on." In the end, he is saved by his directness: "I reached in and got the plums."

Of course, the plums embody his art, as they allude, also, to the larger world of modern poetry and its other famous plums; what I want to say, however, is this: Stafford uses the poem to examine his life, not to defend it.

Being disinterested means more than going without fear; it means going where the material goes, whether to Paris or the fridge. Glibness celebrates easy conclusions; disinterested writing celebrates things as they are. "The satisfaction of the hunger," scholar Helen White has written, "the final justification of experience, is to be found in the experience itself.... The contemplation of the object and not its conquest or use toward some other end, that is the purpose." Creative writing workshops, Bly and Loveland tell us, often train young writers to write for audience approval — the workshop, in their case — which means to write for assent.

The larger culture remains suspicious toward art because art succeeds only to the degree that it abandons self-justification and wishful thinking — the qualities of assertions that often drive our general, cultural discourse. Try another magazine if you must have a villain. If you think the speaker in the poem by Allison Eir Jenks sits, figuratively, between churchgoers and her alcoholic mother because she rejects them, you are wrong. She is not uninterested. She is disinterested. She loves them both.

THE LORD IS EASY TO PLEASE

Allison Eir Jenks

"Hope, Lord. Feed Me Hope, Lord, Or Break My Teeth."
--Olena Davis

I live off the parking lot of Grace Church
and drink coffee at noon on my front steps,
still wrinkled in last night's diva dress.
Today the preacher's sign reads,
Life is a gift. Love is life.

Every Sunday, people still dress up for God,
their hair curled up like roses,
bodies drenched in the scent of faith—
sour and dramatic, always blooming.
God's alphabet is everywhere.

The crossing guard's body is a cross.
The intersection is a cross
where the elderly hold each other up.
I wish they'd come over
and summon me to unveil,

to let God know where I stand.
But they don't notice me across the grass,
inhaling their exhaust fumes—
childless, unmarried, half-drunk
on last night's good sins.

I suppose I didn't have to
flash the truck driver,
or spank that old security guard.
There is something about every man
and woman that makes me want to kiss them.

The doors have shut. Prayer is private.
All the believers are singing

the apologies of my childhood,
memorized while mustached nuns
clenched my ankles to measure my uniform—

how sorry I was for cutting off a piece
of my father's girlfriend's hair,
for the nun who got in trouble
for her pistol collection,
used to hunt deer and duck;

for wanting to climb Jack's penis
because I heard it could unravel
like a serpent and grow taller than him.
And I was sorry for wanting to steal his beanstalk
and use it as a ladder to sneak up on God

and get the damn truth.
I was brimming with faith.
But now I can't remember much more
than God's multiplication tables—
how we counted pine cones

and spread them across the floor.
I never wanted them to stop multiplying.
I bit into one with the hope I would grow
into the tree from which pine cones
infinitely fell and kept growing back.

And I was sorry for my my mother,
who sang into a bottle of Scotch for the Lord
to buy her a Mercedes Benz. But years later
when she came home driving one,
I knew the lord was easy to please.

I am not brave enough to believe
there is a father more grand than any earth-father
or a lover who would not pin himself up
and die again and again, whose ghost
will have holy wine delivered to my door.

But I do admire
the last of the divine old people
who never forgot their prayers,
for wanting to be loved
like no one could love them on earth.

Typhoon

When Joseph Conrad described a typhoon, he said very little about towering waves, or darkness, or the whistling of the wind in the shrouds.
                              — Antoine de Saint-Exupéry

I visited the Florida Keys two days before Hurricane Andrew went through, in 1992. Virtually oblivious to danger, blissful among the brisk winds and breakers, I turned around, drove north, and caught a flight home with nothing more than a tourist's appreciation for the potential of human desperation. In the draft of a poem about that drive through the Keys, I wrote, "The sky walks right in / to homes with a bucket / of water for Miami, the rot / of mangroves in marshes along Highway One."

Those lines seem to me now, since Hurricane Katrina and the Indian Ocean tsunami, or mud slides in Washington state, as the kind of poeticized and ultimately phony language that betrays someone who never got waist deep in the actual flood — like the flood that covered much of the Gulf coast this season, whatever flood one meets. The event could as well be a forest fire, which a poet friend recently faced in the Idaho mountains. The world offers us all the authentic experiences we can handle, from political to family-centered typhoons; easy, conventional language won't stand up to authentic human suffering, or its heroism.

It happens — not by coincidence, I hope — that this issue of *New Letters* has something to show us about human desperation and its transcendence. "I am scared," writes Mia Leonin in "John the Baptist," the essay that opens the issue. "I am terrified that I have died or that I've never lived a real moment but in the sleeve of one of Jesus' parables." She is on the bus in Bogotá, Colombia, and, as a writer, she has just comprehended what Robert Day describes in his own essay included here, "The Committee to Save the World." "I am not a 'thinker,'" Day insists. "Nor am I a 'problem solver.' . . . I am by nature a story teller. That is, stories happen to me."

In just that way, Mia Leonin's essay sets the course for everything that follows in this little discussion, which is global in its concern, moral in its desire. We need journalists to rescue the facts of events; but in their furious speed, called communications, journalists during Katrina reached too often into their journalese tool kits to describe the storm "packing" 160-mph winds, and the coast's "deteriorating conditions." Gas prices would, guess what, "spike"; journalists tucked away in Washington, D.C., would tell us about "the rising tide" of crime, "the fire storm" of criticism; and I would think of my own poor, poetic lines about Andrew. The writer who flew home two days before the flood has nothing in common with the frail grandmother who fought for her life in the wash of a New Orleans street. To echo Saint-Exupéry, the grandmother was much too busy.

"There is nothing dramatic in the world, nothing pathetic, except in human relations," writes Saint-Exupéry in *Wind, Sand, and Stars*. That is the moral imperative of literary writing. "The physical drama cannot touch us until someone points out its spiritual sense." The literature of a typhoon builds slowly, out of a gesture. We ask of our great writers to stay in the storm awhile, to get a feel for it.

"Rising up between the cracked sidewalks and the thick clouds of smoke overhead," writes Mia Leonin, about the homeless people of Bogotá, "they stride purposefully down the median with capes of burlap sacks and random scraps of fabric flying behind them." When writers step off the paved walkways of conventional prose, stories happen to us.

Glory

> *There are those minds who cannot feel people, or cannot under-stand people of different points of view, and who are profoundly moved only by some ideological theme. Those persons I think can never become great novelists.*
> — Pearl S. Buck, *University Review (New Letters)*, 1936

I sometimes like to read aloud Henry V's St. Crispin's Day speech, which, as Shakespeare has it, roused English troops to defeat the French, on French soil, October 25, 1415, at Agincourt. Were I about to go into battle, that speech would work for me, I like to believe; and I'd be grateful for it. The means of salvation for a soldier is victory, and victory likes things simple. Instead of air support, Henry had archers.

On a recent Memorial Day, versions of that speech gave many of us the prescribed glow. Yet on TV, one could not ignore certain contrasts: On one channel, fighter jets soared to the National Anthem, and "Hometown Heroes" saluted; on another channel, Oliver Stone's *Platoon* had soldiers fragging their comrades, some gone virtually insane. "No, I lied," Sherman Alexie says in a poem "The Gathering Storm," to mock the rhetoric of denials. "There was no wind and no trees, / No storm, no thunder, no lightning, no knives."

I came of age during the Vietnam War and remember Secretary of Defense Robert McNamara's version of Henry V's speech, in the form of an article in *Reader's Digest*. He detailed, with considerably less flare, the "domino theory" that was meant to alert us to the global communist threat and justify our stand in Southeast Asia; later, in 1995, he published a memoir, *In Retrospect*, apologizing for his trickery and for leading us into the trenches, over and over. He wanted his book to be more history than tragedy, though, in retrospect; he had learned, as with certain mystics, that human experience is self-made. Tragedy has a personal bite. Each generation seems to strip its sleeves, show its scars; and writers must tell the stories.

Literary writing achieves power to the degree it sets aside presumption and ideology. Imagine the poems of Diana O'Hehir, how they live: "Last night I dreamed my hands were back." She's writing about the speaker's hands, not terror and war. The poems that matter to me generally take a personal view. A fortune-cookie message seems to say, along with St. Paul to the Galatians, "Whatsoever a man soweth, that shall he also reap." On Memorial Day, we sow a bit of glory and a bit of death. Art seeks another choice. It asks us to experience other individuals as ourselves. In this way, literature toughens us, as Sherman Alexie has written, "because it's easy to lie about death."

Form

Energy is Eternal Delight.
— William Blake

Writing that is too soft-hearted will not save us. Consider the nature of the prose sentence — its narrative devices, characterization, poetic imagery, metaphorical leaps, and its particular obligations set forth by a fidelity to fact. We at *New Letters* take our lead from one of today's authorities on the personal essay, Phillip Lopate, who once offered the following advice for essayists: "Unless one begins to turn the material over and find something that goes against the grain of conventional thinking, or that implicates oneself more deeply in an ironic, complex vision, it is probably — sad to say — going to turn out dull and trite on the page."

Lopate's advice disregards subject and focuses entirely upon the writer's character, the writer's ability to get beyond his or her self-interests, self-absorbed ideas, and let experience lead the way. Lopate's injunction, to go against the grain of conventional thinking, drives the structural integrity of the contemporary essay. It turns the essay against the assertion of ideas and toward narrative, which humbles us.

The term *essay*, for fact-based prose, has an elegance not found, to my ear, in the term "creative nonfiction," or CNF, in the trade short form. Other terms roughly synonymous — "literary journalism," "new journalism," "personal essay" — do not encompass enough range for what the essay can do. One quality that makes an essay fresh must be its immediacy, its desire less to analyze experience than to be the experience. Among the essays I have loved from *New Letters* over the years, a reader would be asked to fly an airplane upside down, perform surgery, hike a mountain in Spain, run for her life.

Yet I follow that statement with a caution. What matters about the essay is not so much what is said but how the writer says it. I can point to the first sentence of "On Being Cool," by Laurence Gonzales, to illustrate at least three principles important to the art of the essay and, more crucially, a sentence.

> When I was a boy, kicking around the dying oil fields of southeast Texas with my grandfather's .22 rifle and a stolen package of Chesterfields, I had the idea that the highest achievement in coolness would be to fly an airplane upside down.

The sentence performs the hard, journalistic work of laying out time and place, while suspending its own punch line. It introduces, in its second half, the dual topics of the overall essay — flying and being cool — and in that sweep, it measures the character of the writer by drawing attention away from the speaker as the essay's primary focus. Finally, the most vivid and eccentric image in the sentence arrives at its very end, as if to assure us, as Phillip Lopate suggests, that we seek an ironic and complex vision. So it is for any good essay, designed to displace our complacency and to show us — in private or public ways — how a single sentence can get work done. In the world of sentences, that is what toughness looks like.

"All That I Remember"

— Countee Cullen

Horses would not seem to mean much to someone like me. I grew up in the city of St. Louis, where we negotiated buses, hopped on bicycles or motorcycles, sat in traffic, cut through alleys, and parked our cars in backyards along North Grand Avenue to attend Cardinals' games at old Busch Stadium (the stadium before the stadium just demolished). Until recent years — when I seem always to be meeting people who ride, or own, or bet on, or study horses, or have kids who do — I had only one encounter with those house-high creatures; and that encounter has been returning more and more to memory. At age 9 or maybe 12, in the late 1950s, my best friend, Johnny McCarthy, and I decided we wanted nothing more than to be around horses; so we approached the supervisor at the stables in Forest Park, St. Louis' grand city park, and volunteered for the only kind of work we imagined we were qualified to do, shoveling manure.

I remember the man's disdain for our offer, and how he told us that we actually did not qualify for the job. We were white boys. Shoveling manure was a job for another kind of boy; and, judging from the man's tone, we should have known that. I won't quote here the man's perfectly succinct, declarative sentence, but, like the boy in the poem "Incident" by Countee Cullen — who rode "in old Baltimore" from May until December — that sentence is one I always will remember.

In Daniel Woodrell's "The Horse in Our History," from *New Letters,* an elder presents some historical details to the story's young narrator and then yells at him, "Don't write that." The presence of horses in this issue — here more by coincidence than design — takes us the slow way to the tip of a gravel road, to the horizon, where we can speak or write what's needed. Art is about exposures; and the process of creating a story, a poem, or a life, inevitably must come to confront those details that brought us to the present state.

What my and Woodrell's stories have to do with art goes well beyond the task of knowing what a horse is — as Dickens' schoolteacher Thomas Gradgrind would demand of girl number 20 — and attempts to understand what an artist is. This issue of the magazine also includes representative art canvases of words and drawings by the poet Mark Strand, in which Strand writes out in longhand each draft of a particular poem, with intermittent sketches of images from the poem, and arrives in the bottom right corner of his canvas with the finished poem.

Fellow poet Jorie Graham discusses the process in "The Art of Revising," her lyrical essay about Strand's work. As with Countee Cullen's memory of Baltimore, or my memory from the other end of racism, Jorie Graham sees the process of revision as one that confronts, suppresses, and finally exposes the web of associations created in the creation of art — the submerged bits of memory and connections not always visible in the finished work or, I want to say, in the persons we are. "We are watching a life," she says. The miracle of simultaneity, as Graham describes Mark Strand's canvases, amounts to, in her words, "a moving erasure without being able to erase the exposures such erasures erased."

Every poem, story, essay we write confronts that erasure-and-revelation process. In its most basic sense, a memory dredged up from the past, or a dream, reveals some part of the process that results in this, the art, and perhaps the human being. Mark Strand's distinctive contribution is to fix every point of the process in time, on a single canvas. "Each drawing [of breath, of line]," Jorie Graham says, "remains side by side, in spite of time."

All art is a celebration. Readers sometimes lose sight of that because artists and writers must be willing to face everything, even evil and tragedy. They write it. Artists, by their nature, I believe, do not turn away. "The body fell within a shout of a house that still stands," reads the opening sentence of Woodrell's story. What took us there? Where will it lead? When the elder in the story explains to Woodrell's narrator, "These were not men lamed by any sorts of doubts about anything they did," I hear that stable manager again in my mind. Maybe my editorial decisions come from such experience. In each story or poem I read in manuscript, I can't help but seek to confront some moral dilemma. For me, that's the story.

"Bench 1," tape on *National Geographics*, a sculpture art by Garry Noland

Art + Work

1.

Garry Noland sweeps a pile of trash across his studio floor, and I am reminded that making art is work not worship (Don't be ridiculous), though the work may depart normal reason and common sense. For us who come from blue-collar families — laborers, wood choppers, ditch diggers, furnace installers, land graders — the twinge of being foolish never quite escapes our senses whenever we get involved with art.

Garry Noland pushes the broom. He clears territories, which could be the dimensions and zones of a metaphor: the artist as homesteader. Take Noland Road north toward Independence, Mo., for example, where his family arrived in the 1820s, then to the "new house," built by grandparents Herb and Dora Noland in 1948, where the Nolands live; or go to his studio in the working world of the West Bottoms, Kansas City, and you will find saws, wires, old TVs, window fans, rivet guns, and, yes, duct tape. You will find several wall-like structures, which he calls "Benches," roughly and totteringly each 3-feet high, maybe 5-feet long, made of multi-colored blocks covered in duct tape, held together solely by their own weight and design. Call this the art of unsteadiness amidst the contraries of place and movement. Noland has given each wall self-retainability, dependent on its composition and mass alone, like a slope of earth that also could sag and fail due to a quake, rain, gravity, or earth's hidden energy.

2.

The colorful duct-taped blocks flow like brush strokes. I never had seen such a pallet. When I worked in the heating, cooling, and plumbing industry, we had battleship gray or brown duct tape for handle grips and temporary seals; our dreams did not conceive of silver-lining, blue-bath, or canary colors. It would have been ludicrous, as in the Latin *ludus*, meaning sportive. Joking around.

From work-a-day people many artists come. When playing the critic, as does Howard Nemerov in "The Painter Dreaming in the Scholar's House" about Paul Klee, I also often look for sensible images, "mountain, flower, cloud, and tree, / All haunted there as of a human face." Yet, one might as well look for the secrets of the universe. Respect must be paid, both to the known and to the unknown, and, as much as joking around matters in art, one wants to go beyond. Get serious. Now, look at these seasonal markings of the artistic intelligence.

3.

"My mother was a traveler of the mind," Noland says, which means she decoded her imagination through *National Geographic*s, her collection of subscription copies long absorbed, by now, into her son's other art projects; new copies, Garry Noland prospects and heaps onto the warehouse floor, as if mined somewhere. They are a natural resource, these decades of abstractions one needs to wheel in with a hand truck.

Likely, inside one of these works, in one of the adobe-style tiles and bricks of gloss and tape — cut up and covered issues of *National Geographic*s — lies the story of my own grandmother's village, Gibellina Vecchia, destroyed in the 1968 earthquake that shook the valley of the Belice River in central Sicily. Yet in 1997, I did walk its ruined streets, carrying her imagined life. Do I now sit on Garry Noland's "Bench" and follow the mark of his "Endless X," as if it were left for a carpenter's apprentice in the reconstruction project of my ancestral home? Art tells us one thing — to make our world (let me paraphrase Nemerov) and not reconstruct the one before our eyes.

4.

As I write this, news comes of the death of Grace Paley, fiction writer, poet, social activist — it is August 22, 2007 — which compels me to consider the nature of real work. Late in life, believing that the causes and ideals she fought for during the revolutions of the 1960s had lost their force, Grace Paley said, "I don't know where things went wrong, except whatever happens in society, the society corrupts, eats, and takes over. . . . But at the same time there's always this really small little hill of hope that's right in the middle of this."

One cannot miss the association to slope failure in Paley's own distress at the sag in idealistic tendencies, where human aspiration, itself, is subject to what the poet Shelley, in "Hymn to Intellectual Beauty," recognizes when "The awful shadow of some unseen Power / Floats through unseen among us." Paley caught herself, as Shelley caught himself later in his poem, and, while neither could deny slope failure of many kinds, each acknowledged, at a crucial moment, an ascendant "hill of hope." You still can see, Paley went on to say, people doing wonderful things. To build, anyway, among unsteadiness, that's the work of the artist. It takes courage to do wonderful things.

5.

The transaction between *National Geographic*s and these sculptures dramatizes the invisible power, awful and wonderful, Shelley wrote of. Garry Noland might color-code the history of the planet into blocks that form the alphabet in Morse Code, or radiate waves of earth and light, and lay them in a wall, as if connections to these structures and drawings were everywhere and without exception. One cannot anticipate the nature of homesteadedness. Yes, in 1985 the architect Francesco Venezia created a homage to my grandmother's village by asserting its ascendance in the new settlement, Gibellina Nuova, and installing fragments of the ruins into walls of the new village.

"The fragment is set in a wall rhythmically scanned by courses of yellow sandstone," Venezia wrote at the time, "with alternately plain and patterned faces. To emphasize the sense of the ruin's arrival in its new location, the whole stone facade rests on a plinth of concrete with a projecting molding whose shadow . . . accentuates that sense of detachment, almost levitation, of the gigantic wall screen."

6.

In my visits to Noland's studio, I kneeled on the floor — got on my hands and knees — among the layers of these little, weighty walls. They nearly levitated, bigger than I am, to use a geology association from Noland, himself, like little landslides, or road cuts. Had they merely transported me to the old country, and my immigrant links, or to the landscape of my home state, Missouri, I would have had to admit a touch of morbidity. That is, the limitation of a solely physical existence. The event, however, seemed to have shrunk me down among the lines of a poem, off normal scale, feeling not foolish at all. As the critic Gaston Bachelard has pointed out, a linear reading alone deprives us of countless daydreams.

I believe Garry Noland actually hoped that I would knock over one of his slopes, his walls, his line works, and be done with the sanctimony that sometimes attends fine art. I did not, still faithful to my working-class past, respecting another person's job, being careful; I did, in some way, however, enter the secret alphabet of the imagination, perhaps even the mindfulness of all things, as Howard Nemerov says in his poem, "As though spirit and sense were not at odds." We are to look a little beyond the face of the artwork here, I think, neither to the timeless moment nor the physical work. There is something worshipful in that.

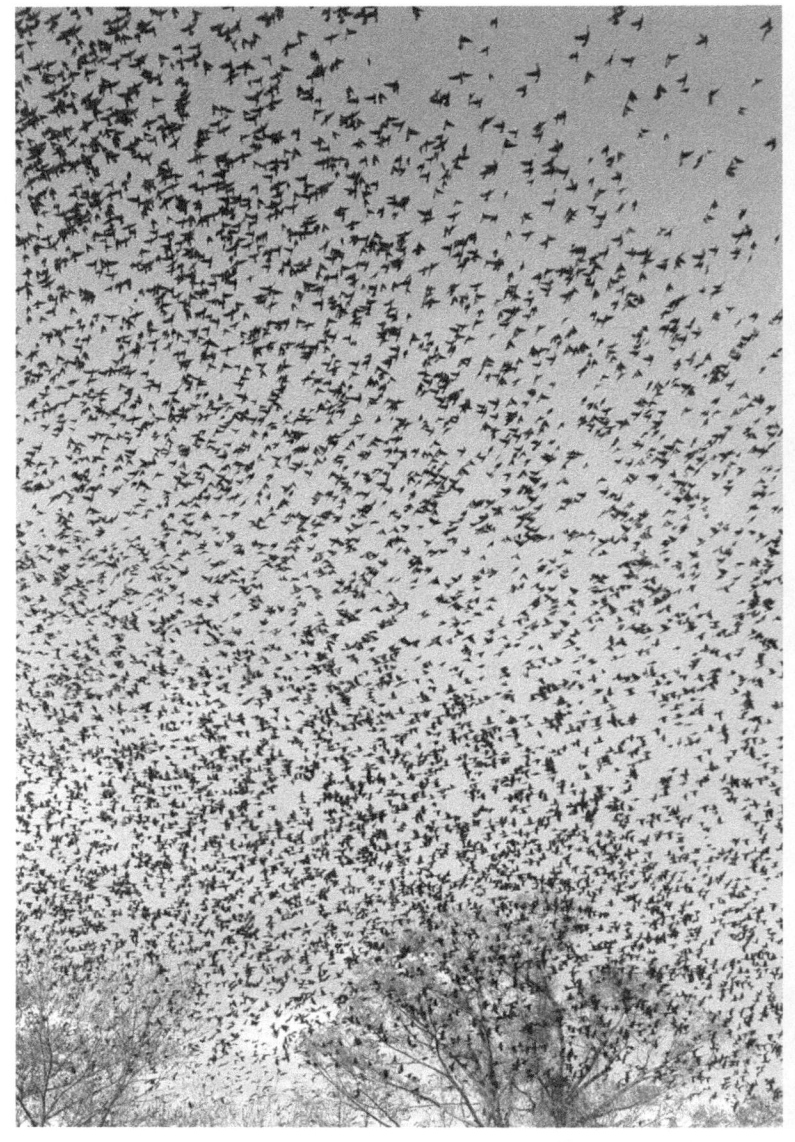

"Red-wing Blackbirds," photograph by Roi J. Tamkin (*original in color*)

Fast and Slow

Look at the cover photo of this issue of *New Letters*. Each red-winged blackbird, rising and swirling into the sky, contains the spirit of a writer or artist who once published work in these pages. Think of it. Never-before-seen writing and art, over the past 77 years, from the wing tips of Edgar Lee Masters, Diego Rivera, Pearl S. Buck, Countee Cullen, May Swenson, J. D. Salinger, Mbembe Milton Smith, William Carlos Williams, Grant Wood, E. E. Cummings, Elizabeth "Grandma" Layton, Gwendolyn Brooks, Crystal Field, Vincent O. Carter, Richard Wright. All birds.

Birds might be fleeting; life might be fleeting; great literature, however, stays around a while. It might not have the same popular sweep as Twitter, or the turmoil of *Time*, but this literary journal does something just as important: It allows readers to wonder, to step away from the world of the paid political ad or the diatribe, into a considered experience.

From the audience recently, where I sat at the downtown public library in Kansas City, a man asked the visiting speaker, Joyce Carol Oates, how she managed to write her many books all in longhand, a technique she just had revealed. "My mind thinks faster than my hand can write," said the man. "I need a computer keyboard to keep up with my thoughts." A general assent seemed to puff across the audience.

The question highlighted a feature — call it a value — of literary art, not always or easily acknowledged: Literature slows us down. Here was an author, Ms. Oates, emblematic in our culture for high productivity, who had just baffled the crowd by her adherence to the human-scale, physical, scratching out of one sentence after another, although she happens to do so, she pointed out, hour after hour, day after day. Of her slow method, she made a joke, citing another writer, Shakespeare, who also worked in longhand, and, of course, might be said to have had a fairly quick mind.

Shakespeare, let's admit, might have worked by computer if he could have, but the point has been made by the work, itself. It holds up. It rewards patience. I don't know how many readers will see our opening essay, "Eternal 48 Hours," by Raad ABDUL-AZIZ; but the impact of a man's captivity in Iraq and his meditation on family cannot be measured in hits. The essay can be measured only in time. The eccentricities of technique — typing, handwriting, dictating — do not determine the value of literary art, which reveals itself only carefully, only gradually. "There is a secret bond between slowness and memory," Milan Kundera has written, "between speed and forgetting." The fact that the souls of our past writers live on in the red-winged blackbirds on the cover of this magazine should be proof enough that literary art carries itself forward, not to be forgotten.

Service

John Barth, in a 1989 eulogy, extolled Donald Barthelme as a good "literary citizen," citing Barthelme's service with PEN American Center and other organizations. Kate Gale, a recent president of PEN Center USA, teaches seminars on how writers can help support other writers: write blurbs, produce readings, serve on boards. The poet Robin Becker makes literary citizenship part of her teaching, which includes encouraging students to review new books of poems and to send the reviews to magazines, such as *New Letters*, to publish, which we have done.

To provide service means that you stand publicly for something you believe to have fundamental, intrinsic value. Critic Roberto Calasso calls one such value "absolute literature," which means, in part, "unbound," writing, as he says, "freed from any duty or common cause, from any social utility." Implied in that is a spiritual component to both writing and service; we do it for its own sake.

The concept of literary service gets too little play, in my view, even though we live among great examples. Within a few weeks of each other, this magazine lost a number of friends and literary laborers — the essayist and fiction writer Donn Irving Blevins; the poet Michael Paul Novak; former U.S. Senator Thomas Eagleton; critic and teacher Mary Reefer. They organized readings, mentored writers, advocated for the arts. They were people who measured up, in the words of critic Cynthia Ozick, to their "public responsibility" as commentators on art and culture, as citizens who were honest, fair, and, perhaps most important, selfless.

Please don't diminish the notion of literary service by

invoking conventional pieties. I even now can hear someone whisper the phrase "labor of love." Let's call this real work. It's a labor of determination, labor of acceptance, labor of transcendence.

Time and the Fabric of Immensity

The title of this note seemed to bash into my head one morning this May, while I looked out toward thunderstorms that were, themselves, scheduled to bash this wheat-belt region of the country for the next five days at least. It so happens, I was re-reading *Don Quixote* and, un-Quixote like, pondering where this magazine should be headed, given its 2008 National Magazine Award for the Essay. The magazine industry, itself, including other editors of top-tier literary magazines, seems to consider this award best in the field; and I am, at this moment, happy to accept that assessment. Don't think too much, Quixote might say, but do stand for some value. From him, we might learn principles of life, mission, and vocation. "He rode on his way," Cervantes tells us, "going where it pleased his horse to carry him, for he believed that in this consisted the very soul of adventure."

The very soul of adventure. What did it mean, then, for me to say in my acceptance "speech" to the audience at Lincoln Center on May 1st, that the mission of a literary magazine differs in quality from that of many other, even other fine, magazines? I know I said that because friends who were present tell me so. I actually remember only a few things: jumping from my seat and screaming when awards presenter, Charlie Rose, announced the winner, "*New Letters*"; Thomas E. Kennedy, our winning essayist, giving me a hug and then screwing on his trademark leopard-skin, pill-box hat; all of us on stage shaking hands; and then me, staring at the microphone and taking a breath to speak. What came out, as far as I know, was gibberish; but friends who were present tell me I said that the mission of a literary magazine is to advance literary art itself.

Whom did I think I was? In the audience were some of the great editors of our time, including Lewis H. Lapham, Katrina vanden Heuvel, David Remnick, Tina Brown, and my friend Stephen Corey; yet, evidently, on I plunged, asserting the value of our peculiar task. Fortunately, Thomas Kennedy's winning essay, "I Am Joe's Prostate," offered the solution, variously described by the American Society of Magazine Editors as "wince inducing," "outrageously honest," and "wickedly funny." I described the essay as terrifying and hilarious. Any time writing can be described only in paradoxical terms, we're approaching literary art.

So it is, we move forward on principles that set literary writing into the category of adventure, meaning that we almost cannot prepare for it. It sets us off in a new way. One of our *New Letters* writers, Robert Olen Butler, states in his own book about writing, *From Where You Dream*, a basic principle of literary art, which he takes from film director Akira Kurosawa: "To be an artist means never to avert your eyes." Theoretical writing, full of concepts and ideas, softens experience into tidy abstractions. Writing of direct experience — no matter how distasteful or unusual — enlarges our stature, gives us life.

Do not look away, then, from Janset Berkok Shami's short story here, which begins, "Recently I had a slightly retarded lover." Many of our readers averted their eyes from "I Am Joe's Prostate," and referred to its topic as "sketchy" (in the sense of being unsafe or not right), in the sense of being out of place for a literary magazine. I know. I needed to ask myself the big question, as well: Is it literary? Then, as now, I had to assess what I mean by literary.

So I turn to Quixote: "The Knight-errant . . . endures the fierce rays of the sun in uninhabited deserts, the inclemency of wind and ice in winter." The storms this May tell me of the immensity of the individual: "Lions cannot daunt him or demons affright or dragons, for to seek, assault, and overcome such is the whole business of his life, and true office." Yes, earlier in this collection, we heard the philosopher Mencius say, *I hate glibness*, so let's not assume Kennedy, in confronting a medical misdiagnosis, went blissfully undaunted. Yet through his resilience, he transformed the experience from fear of death to love of life.

Take a look at the poem "Woodbridge," by Mary Crockett Hill, where the speaker confronts the arrival of bulldozers and sewage funnels at a cow pasture soon to be developed near her home. "It has such romance in its silver," she says of one huge metal tube, "it seems a passage / to something exceedingly rare." The poet understands time and immensity as a quality of value, beyond the spot in the pasture where, she says, "my teenage boyfriend humped me one chilled night / oblivious to the damp of our toes." The language turns loss to glee, as, for Kennedy, it turns medical trials to the soul of adventure.

In that way, our National Magazine Award tells me — which is something I am told I tried to tell the audience at Lincoln Center — good, literary writing trumps everything. It carries us along and expands our scope. We readers merely need to have courage equal to that required to write it. Didn't we laugh at Quixote, also? Yes. His story is terrifying and hilarious.

WOODBRIDGE

Mary Crockett Hill

Peep frogs going off like sirens
in the field that will not long be a field.

Three bulldozers this week, a Porta-John, a freshly graveled road.

In the brown past dusk, the huge metal tube
that will funnel sewage
has such romance in its silver
it seems a passage
to something exceedingly rare—
a spiraling light
or colony of thumb-sized trolls. . . .

With rain, with spring, with the seed
of a new child in my womb, I am better prepared
to lose this pasture that was never mine.

Twenty-six tidy new houses—full of the stuff that fills houses,
the La-Z-Boys and breakfast stools and liquid soap—
will sit there and there, where the cows bleated and roamed,
where my teenage boyfriend humped me one chilled night,
oblivious to the damp of our toes.

There was always the cow pasture, always the option
of walking westward through the fields into unnamed mountains beyond.

Even if we never walked it. Even if we just stayed home.

Literary Values

> *Literary reading is a popular but declining leisure activity, reaching about one-half of the adult population.*
> — National Endowment for the Arts survey
> "Reading at Risk"

I am not discouraged. Before the release of the 2004 National Endowment for the Arts report "Reading at Risk: A Survey of Literary Reading in America," if you would have asked me how many adults in the United States read poetry as a leisure activity, I would not have guessed 25 million.

To me, that's a lot, but the figure must be read in its most generous sense, to include people drawn by a *New Yorker* cartoon to the same page as a Jack Gilbert poem. Lucky them. They might have read just that one poem all year. That's enough. The N.E.A. survey nevertheless shows a decline in the percentage of the U.S. adult population that reads literature — from 56.9 percent in 1982, to 54.0 in 1992, to 50.2 in 2002, to 46.9 in 2012 — where *literature* and *reading* are defined as any single poem, play, or work of fiction, without regard to genre or quality, as long as the reading was done as an option and not as a school or job requirement.

Strangely, in each year of the first decade of the 21st century, *New Letters*, a literary magazine, annually increased its readership. The way our audience has grown at *New Letters* tells us something about readers in this country, in a way that circumvents survey numbers. Large numbers of people continue to value literary experience, the life of reading and its slower pace. Our job at the magazine has been to say to as many people as we can, "It is still acceptable, still valuable."

Not long ago, public transportation, for example, was

habitat for readers. On a train, bus, airplane, the door would close and one could see books and magazines opening like petals of flowers in people's palms, up and down the aisle — a kind of imposed time out from our connected, pragmatic lives. The glow of a tablet screen notwithstanding, literature requires us to slow down, be quiet, contemplate relationships. The people who want a literary magazine would seem to want that slowness, that contemplatory experience.

The questions have come up, however: What difference does it make? So what if fewer people read writers such as Mary Gordon, Hilary Masters, Robert Day, Gladys Swan? Psychologist James Hillman, citing Confucius, has written that the rectification of society starts with the rectification of its language. Laws and programs begin in words, and if the words of our leaders, Hillman says, are entangled in garbled speech, intoned in nasal whining, bereft of inspiration and wit, and flatter than the commercials that surround them, then we can't expect society to advance.

I rest my case.

Actually, I don't, because Hillman's comments suggest that literature is important because it is useful to good legislation and social programs. It is not. If that were the case, we could throw away a few things, such as "Thirteen Ways of Looking at a Blackbird." We could even throw away the blackbird. Literature exists as a seedbed for individual thinking, for its own sake. Literature is not a defense of freedom or a means of achieving freedom. A work of literature is the freedom.

People often try to justify literature by giving it some practical use — one way is the habit of searching for themes in literary writing, as if a story were simply a key to answering some of life's vexing problems. Literature might do that, but so might a diet book or political memoir. Literary writing, my friends, resists purposefulness as a goal; it cannot be confused with a book called *Shakespeare in Charge: The Bard's Guide to Leading and Succeeding in Business*, with cover blurbs that praise Shakespeare's practical advice, by Colin Powell and Warren Buffett.

Literary writing often doesn't get us anywhere at all, except perhaps deeper into our selves, beauty, empathy, and amazement, those qualities that run against the grain of contemporary America. In a 2004 *Harper's* essay "Quitting the Paint Factory," subtitled "On the virtues of idleness," Mark Slouka points out this very dilemma: "What we are leaving behind today, at record pace," he writes, "is whatever belief we might once have had in the value of unstructured time: in the importance of uninterrupted conversation, in the beauty of play. In the thing in itself — unmediated, leading nowhere."

God bless arts advocates who composed the term "arts industry," for that is what they believed legislators and business patrons would understand. We accept the term for its benefits, but ultimately, it condescends. There is industry, finance, and sometimes personal advantage to knowing the works of Twain or Woolf; but don't confuse those with the moral force of literary art. At its best and highest, literature creates a kind of solidarity with the human race. As novelist John Gardner has pointed out, "The writer must be not only capable of understanding people different from himself but fascinated by such people."

I recently mentioned this N.E.A. survey to several writers who contribute to *New Letters*. It was not news to them, and they shook it off as they always had done. Writing takes an enormous act of faith. In many cases, writers tell me they have been sustained by a little secret they carry regarding the audience they write for. It is this: A work of literature exists in a continuum beyond present time. It transcends 2005, 2015, even this decade. Literature is greater than the hot book of the week, despite tax laws that force publishers to remainder much of their inventory. Writers often see themselves in the line of Basho and Emily Dickinson, Daniel DeFoe and Martha Gellhorn, Nathaniel Hawthorne and Stephen Crane — the long tradition, where readership accumulates across time, long after the author may cease to be, as this morning I returned to a poem by the 19th-century's John Keats.

At my desk at *New Letters*, I say no to dozens of writers each week, some quickly, some after agonizing deliberation. I don't pander to them or condescend to them. Writers always have known that by sitting alone, composing, dreaming, weaving tales, they risk everything. Hours, years, a lifetime of work could be consigned to oblivion for many reasons, beyond the size of the potential audience; yet some of us imagine success. Some of us continue, as John Gardner has said, "the foolish pastime, the making of real art."

Take This Seriously

*Dante, who knew the world about suffering, had a place in
hell for people who were grave when they might have rejoiced.*
— Marilynne Robinson

You want satire? We've got your satire right here. Irony, sarcasm. Wit. *New Letters* has been stocking up on all varieties since the price went so low in July 2008, when *The New Yorker* ladled up irony on its cover. Remember: a drawing of Michelle and Barack Obama in Islamic and military dress, fist-bumping in the oval office, with an American flag burning in what I still think of as the Nixon fireplace (he reportedly cranked the air-conditioning way down so he could cozy-up to the fire). In any case, *The New Yorker*'s ironic commentary went over as well as a subprime mortgage.

More on *The New Yorker* in a moment. First, a disclaimer. This magazine uses no artificial ingredients. The satire in Mary Jo Bang's new translation of Dante's *The Inferno*, published here, might seem light, delectable, but don't stuff yourself. It's real butter. It will come up on you later. The first circle of hell, my friends, looks a lot like paradise, "a meadow of new green grass," where languish the greatest minds of antiquity — Aristotle, Plato, Democritus, "who says the world is no more / Than happenstance and chance." Could he be wrong? Democritus' lack of faith amounted to a lack of baptism, alone. Blessed be the rational mind, for it shall have paradise in hell.

The thing about irony is this: Once the artist explains it — I did the explaining above, not the poet — irony disappears. Poof. It stops being funny. People walk out on you. If you want to understand, read Mark Twain's "How to Tell a Story." Don't tell us that you're telling us a joke. Barry Blitt's *New Yorker* cover, called "The Politics of Fear," might have hit its unstated target, but not many people cared. Too unstated. The target: demagogues who depict the Obamas as secretively unAmerican, patriotically suspect.

"A joke's a very serious thing," wrote 18th-century British poet Charles Churchill. Most serious of all, however, were left-leaning Obama supporters, some intellectuals and artists, who said the cover cartoon failed precisely because it did not explain itself. It risked being misunderstood and thereby would scare away voters for Obama. As jokes go, some of us can tell them and some can't; and one award-winning graphic designer, Paula Scher, says the Blitt cartoon simply is not outrageous enough. Another political cartoonist once said in a lecture I attended that if his audience doesn't get the joke in three seconds, he has failed. Several artists and at least one professional comic said they wished the cartoon had a chubby little Karl Rove resting on the couch, a giant thought balloon growing from his head, in which the cartoon of the Obamas would reside. Then the meaning would be clear, entirely serious in media terms.

I heard that explanation repeatedly, as to why so many people thought the cartoon tasteless — to which I answer, Hell is tasteless. Dante nevertheless wrote it up, using some bit of irony. We have to work out our own salvation, it says somewhere, with fear and trembling. This small essay cares to defend simply this: our ability to say one thing and mean another. The presidential election matters greatly, but we must first of all demand of ourselves that we face our frailties, our failures, and make of them a bit of fun.

"*The New Yorker* may think," said Bill Burton, press secretary for Obama's campaign ". . . that their [sic] cover is a satirical lampoon of the caricature Senator Obama's right-wing critics have tried to create, but most readers will see it as tasteless and offensive. And we agree." Actually, only most

Democrats found it offensive — 70 percent, according to a Pew Research Center poll of July 24, 2008. So it goes in postmodern life that only 48-percent of Republicans, the intended targets of the satire, felt the snub. The joke backfired.

At the core of all this is the reason Kim Addonizio's essay and Albert Goldbarth's poetry from this magazine take on the dangers of wit and implication. We do weird things, artists and writers, willing to *embrace the stink of barnacles*, as Goldbarth suggests, and *the royal jelly of delight*. What we have here in our culture, in our popular media — to risk sounding elitist — is fear of communicating on different kinds of levels. What Mr. Burton finds offensive is the irony, not the message. He loves the message, but he is afraid to say in public that he loves the irony. Therefore, he must appear to publicly hate the message. Ironic, huh?

"Flatwater II," painting by Lisa Grossman (*original in color*)

Power

Power twists and turns. Look down from the heavens onto the mighty rivulets. They reach everywhere. Harmony Neal, in her essay "She Don't Lie," confronts the power of her own name — both her original name, Cocaine, and her redirected name, Harmony — and what type of control her mother might have wanted to impose by the first name. Credit, perhaps, the ideology of the times, the culture of the '60s. Behind each name, it seems, lies a great force.

A philosophy professor of mine at the University of Missouri-Columbia, years ago, said in class that he considered the first principle of the universe to be power, itself. We had been discussing the poem "Burnt Norton," the first of T. S. Eliot's "Four Quartets," which places us humans, says Eliot, "At the still point of the turning world. / Neither flesh nor fleshless; Neither from nor toward." Eliot's "dance," meaning the life we experience, takes place at the point between past and future. Power appears, as in art, in the moment; yet we're told, "Do not call it fixity." This was a philosophy class, after all, not literature or religion; and I was there in hopes, young as I was, of consolation, a sense of direction.

The professor's comment about power came as a flash and expanded in my thoughts, largely because I did not want it to be so. I wanted love or virtue, even justice, to show the way. Yet Eliot says, in his cryptic style, "Love is itself unmoving." Like most young people then, I identified with the sensitive, tentative Prufrock. Him, I could understand. I could understand, also, Eliot's position that only God stands outside of time's still point, raised as I was in the Catholic faith. I went to church, listened to the Jesuits, got lost in body in South

America; once, in Equador, having come upon a man with a semi-automatic rifle on a dark road, whistled my way past, powerless and blessed.

Lately, power seems the prevalent message, physically in earthquakes and tsunamis, and in the affected nuclear-fuel rods, unsteady in our care, as they seem inevitably to be. Materialist logic intervenes, and, in Wisconsin, Governor Scott Walker succeeded in stripping state workers of nearly all of their collective-bargaining rights (their power) because at this still point in time, he has the power to do so. That outcome seemed little affected by notions of workers' rights, justice, even economics, all duly debated. The U.S. House of Representatives can push to eliminate government support for public broadcasting for the same reason — it has the political power, right now.

Right now. We learn all we need from George Orwell's police officer in the British colony of Burma, in the classic story "Shooting an Elephant," another tale of power. The police officer, representing the Empire, knew he need not shoot the elephant for any rational or just reason — the animal had calmed down from its episode of "must" — but the people, poor and normally powerless, expected him to shoot it. "I could feel their two thousand wills pressing me forward, irresistibly," the officer says. "And it was at this moment, as I stood there with the rifle in my hands, that I first grasped the hollowness, the futility of the white man's dominion in the East." He realized, moreover, the existence of the still point Eliot describes, in which, "at this moment," the perspective we had of the world shifted, as if he and we readers were hovering above ourselves.

Enter the dance of Wendy Barker's poem "I'm Not Sure the Cherry Tree Is the 'Loveliest of Trees,'" in which she hovers over herself looking at trees and responding to the A. E. Houseman poem "Loveliest of Trees." No wonder we seek the still point. Time holds the power, here. "Since I haven't many springs left," she says, our speaker stops to examine the life she has now over one she might choose — beside "the bodhi tree – under which the Buddha sat," for example, or coconut palms or eucalyptus, to which she submits, in all humility, her immediate experience: "How can I leave?" she asks, rhetorically, near the end of her poem, "our own / Mexican persimmon near the drive." This speaker knows herself, and her answer resolves the impulses that could otherwise lead her away, off center, or at least to distraction.

Because Eliot had the audacity to introduce the notion of spiritual insight into his poem, I suggest it as a way of seeing Barker's poem, also, and other art. The etymology of "holiness" derives from *wholeness* (*to be preserved whole*) — not split apart, not distracted, but grounded and authentic — as Eliot reminds us, "Evacuation of the world of fancy." Art provides us with integrity.

Eliot says in "Burnt Norton,"

> [that] Only by form, the pattern,
> Can words or music reach
> The stillness, as a Chinese jar still
> Moves perpetually in its stillness.

I have only to look at a photograph of one rooster by Terrie Wahling — how the high plains revolve around the amazing bird, much like Wallace Stevens' famous jar in Tennessee — or the horse, or a painting of the Kaw River on the cover of this magazine, to experience the still moment given form. As Albert Goldbarth says in "The Rocks and the Grasses," a poem, "Surely / *some* things make a difference." Yes, they do. Power is not unattainable but is in everything, and in us. "The dust / of outer space," Goldbarth submits, "will continue to lay its annual tonnage / at our doorsteps," yet we are not passive. The question is, how do we express power? Do we encourage one another, build each other up? If art holds its center, the answer should be yes.

I'M NOT SURE THE CHERRY IS THE "LOVELIEST OF TREES"

Wendy Barker

So from the first line of the poem I'm quibbling,
                and I don't even teach this poem now
I'm pushing threescore and ten. All that counting
                Housman has us busy doing, figuring
the speaker's age, and I know in class we'd end up
                focusing on the stanzas with the math. Yet
students never had trouble getting hold
                of the poem's carpe diem message: inhale
the scent of roses while you can. I've never seen
                a flowering cherry, have never known
spring in Washington D.C. or England or
                been invited to a hanami, a party to view
the blooms in Tokyo. But I knew the dogwoods
                lacing my first hesitant steps, have known
white pines' needles gleaming with
                light reflected from a northern lake, and
I've known the palo verdes in the dusty Sonoran
                desert where Rudy, my first boyfriend,
kissed me. And the olives I planted
                with my former husband, shoveling down
into Phoenix hardpan. The eucalyptus
                lifting their astringent scent in the Berkeley
hills where I lay in a carpet of fog-softened leaves, ecstatic
                with a lover. The lemon tree by the front door
of the house where my son was born. I could say
                "with rue my heart is laden" for these and all
the trees I may never see again: banyans and teak,
                neem trees, cinnamon and coconut palms,
the bodhi tree—under which the Buddha sat
                so still. And since I haven't many springs
left in me—a dozen? two?—maybe,
                like the woman diagnosed with terminal
cancer who traveled seven continents
                compiling a life list of eight thousand birds,

I could search out all the trees I've never seen,
                including the blossoming cherry. In California
there's a bristlecone that's lived for almost
                five thousand years, and in Sweden, a spruce
that's lived for close to ten. That woman's travels
                kept her cancer in remission, her doctors
were amazed. But how can I leave our own
                Mexican persimmon near the drive, its peeling
layers of coppery silver bark, its branching
                trunk I can't begin to wrap my arms around.

"The Ideal World of Don Quixote," detail from a mural by Luis Quintanilla
(*original in color*)

Madness

We remember what Don Quixote says of love — *that it makes all things equal* — and in that spirit, our cover and inside pages reproduce sections of *The Don Quixote Frescoes*, by the great Spanish artist Luis Quintanilla, painted in 1940 and 1941 at what was then the University of Kansas City (now the University of Missouri-Kansas City). The Quixote figure in these murals is the likeness of one of my predecessors, Alexander Cappon, editor of this magazine through much of the period from 1938 to 1970. Quixote and Alex Cappon fit well into our impromptu theme, as we celebrate *New Letters* magazine's heritage in its 70th year. Lord Byron has written of Quixote, "His virtue makes him mad." What is virtue? In this issue, Marilyn Kallet's "To My Poem of Hope" addresses the question: "Dear poem, if we look again, /and we must, / we will find scraps, / scrawled words, secret histories." In other words, we will face the truth of events. So I cite Quixote's own words from Part One of Cervantes' novel: "A willful wrong voluntarily and knowingly I never committed to anyone."

Quixote's madness is the madness we aspire to. The mainstream press this season points mostly to the presidential election and to our desire for certainty and solutions. Literature sets us to action, only; it does not promise solutions and does not break its promises. It seeks what Jonis Agee here describes in her essay "Wind-Time, Wolf-Time" as the mystery and magic that affirm all life: "A hand reaching out for the world, then pulling back." If you ask for a poem's five-year plan, the poem will ask you for your five-year plan. Sorry. Literature is the only art form that cannot be experienced on any level passively. It requires your involvement.

In what way do our actions in life matter? That is the

question. The spiritual journey through poems, stories, and essays is your journey. "Never mind apportioning blame," says poet Linda Pastan. In just that spirit, we have Thomas E. Kennedy, in his memoir "In the Dark," coming upon a destitute mother and child during a New York City blackout, and asking, What is my role in the lives of these strangers? When he takes the mother and baby to the great Hotel, The Plaza, and asks for water, he might have been standing out front of a giant windmill, holding a little flashlight or waving its beam of D batteries. We have the very personification of idealism, and we might well ask how to sustain our own visions. Kennedy wants to know why they are turned away, when he, alone, had been welcomed earlier. Here, we have everything that should drive our politics. We have the great questions.

TO MY POEM OF HOPE

Marilyn Kallet

I don't blame you for hope,
for wanting the children
to have survived.
Because their names were not
inscribed in the "minority registration,"
you assumed they had slipped
through the net.
My dear, Horb was a hillbilly dot.
Everyone knew everyone.

Now we find this handwritten entry
by Hedwig Schwarz
in her daily book of prayer:
"On Friday, November 28, 1941
at 5:50 a.m., our dear good daughter
Hilde Sara Lemberger and our dear
good grandson Siegfried Israel Lemberger
moved away from here.
We only wish that God may watch over them
and that they stay well."

Their grandmother kept "Sara" and "Israel"
in case of Nazi eyes.
Mother and son "moved away from here"
in early darkness.
The rooster couldn't crow.

The files reveal that Hilda
and Siegfried, called "Friederle"
were deported "east for labor assignment,"
"that is to say, Riga,"
"declared dead on 4/1/1942."

Für tot erklärt.

Pronounced by anonymous agents
with past participles on their hands.

Dear poem, if we look again,
and we must,
we will find scraps,
scrawled words, secret histories,
the cry between the lines:
"Remember. They called me Freddie.
I was six years old.
Here's what really happened."

Cry of the Renegade

The title of this essay comes from a poem by José Domingo Gómez Rojas, which appeared in *New Letters* in English for the first time. In 1920, Chilean authorities found Gómez Rojas' verses to be subversive and considered the poet an anarchist and, worse, insolent. "I do not have, dear minister," Gómez Rojas told his interrogator, "sufficient moral discipline to assume [the title of anarchist], which I will never merit." At which point, Gómez Rojas, much like the resister Olaf in E. E. Cummings' war poem "i sing of Olaf glad and big," was thrown into a jail, where he died.

This edition of *New Letters* could be said to expose idealists among us. They come as aspirants, mostly, unsure and often humble; they admit to feeling ridiculous at times, as, apparently, it must be. Even Clarissa Hay, "Cassie," tough as they come on the roller-derby track, wants to be part of a big, beautiful vision of the world — Yes, she says, "I want to be part of it" — which is why we love her memoir "Queens of Pain." Photographs of "Occupy" demonstrations in Paris, France, and Kansas City, Mo., foster politics less than expose a certain innocence, the appearance, at least, of naiveté, which seems to have become almost inexplicable in these times. I am reminded of a poem by David Ray, "Stopping Near Highway 80," published in his 1974 collection, *Gathering Firewood*, which ends by asking if the distrustful folk in an Iowa town can teach us anything, "we'd ever want to know / of living lives as gentle as we can."

That ending line has stayed with me since the day I first read it, freshly published. It has not lost its power. On the Internet, one now can find an interview conducted by comedian Stephen Colbert with two Occupy Wall Street participants, a young man, Justin, and a young woman, Ketchup. Televised Oct. 31,

2011, the video has been circulated as proof to some people that Occupy protesters are silly, naive, and whacko. I thought so, too, when I received the video from a friend. I squirmed in my seat when Ketchup identified herself as a "female-bodied person," and when Justin first twinkled his fingers downward to express disagreement with Colbert's mock bluster and wisecracks. Hands in the air, another Occupy gesture, can be seen in our Paris photos, gauging consensus.

There I was, admiring Colbert's wit and averting my eyes from the moon-faced pair, in whom I wanted, really wanted, to put my faith. Say something cutting and witty back, I nearly screamed at the screen. Instead, they sat buoyantly bantering with a professional wag, certainly understanding their own silliness, I believe, and unerring. I felt a great sadness. Please don't tell me they were actors. Or do tell me; it doesn't matter, because fictions also hold truths. To look like a fool, or feel like one, at times, often exposes the idealists among us. "A fool who persists in his folly," William Blake nevertheless asserts, "will become wise." Let us hope.

"Is this restoration?" Janice Harrington asks in her poem "Prairie Blazing Star," in this issue. The wands of the blazing star plants reach upward, as the hands in these Paris photos reach up to express agreement. Surely Albert Goldbarth caught that moment in his opening poem here, "Tables," when the Pentecostal congregation, "having lost / themselves . . . gained a place in something larger / than their selves." I would love to hear Goldbarth spar wits with Colbert, not to assess, as with a political debate, a winner, but to enjoy the brightness of their retorts, the prairie-wide windows of their humor. Let us call this edition of *New Letters* a collection of strong minds and wills applied to the celebration of life, all of it. Under the worst circumstances, Gómez Rojas could not resist sparing wits with his captors, and it cost him everything. If dear, red-haired Ketchup can aspire to a life, as she told Colbert, "where my comfort and happiness are not born of the suffering of others," maybe even that naive, misguided, foolish, renegade of a girl can show some of us a way to *live lives as gentle as we can.*

The Goldilocks Zone

At a public event in Kansas City, in October 2013, the poet Martín Espada mentioned that the first poetry book he ever owned was *The Rubáiyát*, by 11th-century Persian poet and astronomer Omar Khayyám, given to Espada as a boy by his father. As an adult, Espada came upon an astounding collection of over 5,000 editions of *The Rubáiyát*, at the home, as Espada said, "of a doctor in Kansas City." That doctor was E. Grey Dimond, a great friend of *New Letters* magazine's, lover of art and literature, who died on Nov. 3, 2013, at the age of 94. Dr. Dimond's Khayyám collection is housed in his former home, named Diastole, a reference to the normal, recurring period of relaxation of the ventricles of the heart, the pause between contractions.

News of Dr. Dimond's death coincided with publication by the National Academy of Science that at least 8.8-billion planets in our galaxy orbit their own suns, much like our own, and, much like our own planet, reside in something called a "Goldilocks zone" — not too hot, not too cold — conducive to life, to flow, perhaps to thought. I admit to having felt for a moment diminished by such news, the loss of one man's presence and the loss, perhaps, of earth's uniqueness. "How sad a heart," Khayyám wrote, "that does not know how to love / that does not know what it is to be drunk with love."

Dr. Dimond, I believe I can say, would not have felt diminished at the expansive possibilities of galactic life. He was one drunk with love. Witness the home he left for us, now used as a conference center by the University of Missouri-Kansas City and the location, for many years, of the *New Letters* Writing Conference, held in June. Diastole, which he and his late wife, Mary Clark Dimond, built in the mid 1970s, when

Dr. Dimond arrived to start the medical school here, sits on a hill just south of downtown Kansas City. It is filled with art and artifacts collected from around the world, a dazzlement for all attendees when they arrive for our conference. I can hear them telephoning spouses, "When you pick me up, you must come inside and see this place." It is, as its creators intended, uplifting. It contains a third-floor library filled with light, a piano room, a lecture room called the Kiva, and two small apartments where I would house visiting writers before Diastole staff had to put a limit on residents. On travels through Kansas City, writer friends still call for me to set them up in that lovely home with the Japanese garden. If I can, I do.

I am compelled to ponder the value of such a "felicitous setting," as the Dimonds called their place, in the creation of art and writing. Dr. Dimond was no recluse in life, but ran the cardiology department at the University of Kansas in the 1950s, was one of the first Americans to visit Communist China, in 1971, beating President Nixon by six months, and became a friend to Edgar Snow, the first Western journalist to interview Mao Zedong. Dimond's first copy of *The Rubáiyát* once belonged to a hospitalized prostitute, whom a doctor friend of his had treated and fallen in love with in Japan. The woman asked that the doctor read to her daily from the book, her solace, her respite.

In Espada's poem about *The Rubáiyát,* he hides the book inside a Playboy calendar, at age 17, so no one would catch him reading poetry. "Awake," Espada quotes Khayyám in his own poem, "For Morning in the Bowl of Night / has flung the Stone that puts the Stars to Flight." I am connecting the dots, now, and there are many, a kind of star chart that illumines our exposures to art and writing, I think, and how they matter. The contractions I felt at the news of those felicitous planets has eased.

I return often to Wordsworth's definition of poetry, "emotion recollected in tranquility," and remember that tranquility, security, often — perhaps always — serve art in its creation and appreciation. Don't ask me to narrowly define tranquility, just to say we can't survive, as artists, without it. Find it at night under the covers, as did poet Brian Turner, writing in his journal after having engaged in a fire fight during the day in the Iraq war; find it more than 20 years after the war in Vietnam, as did a vet friend and poet, H. C. Palmer, before he could, as he said, "negotiate some brokenness." Don't quantify the terms or time span, or the course of thought. Define it as joy, as does philosopher Rollo May, "the emotion that goes with heightened consciousness."

Take from *New Letters* Edward Hoagland's essay "Hippies and Beats," recollections not always tranquil that he could not have written until the time of tranquility had arrived for him. Likewise Paula Streeter's memoir of her life in Honduras, "Angel and *Animales*," only possible after the settling of those events, years removed. Define tranquility, in Wordsworthian terms, as remission for Lewis Ellingham, but even then, I am guessing.

I am not guessing, however, about the joy emitted in the intensity of writing and art presented here in this magazine. The heart rests once more on "The Day After Sinatra Married Mia Farrow," depicted here in a poem by Joseph Millar, under the dawnwashed sky of the Great Society. This, then, is the real moment of creation, when we pause to build our lives again, in words or deed, to welcome those lovely 8.8-billion planets into our society, waving them in, tired as we might be in the morning, happy as hell.

Faith

Faith. Most people say they have it, which I take to mean, they do have it. I had said for many years that I had no faith, which made my close friends laugh at me and say, of course I did. They could see what I could not. Many years ago, I spotted the poet Robert Bly walking with some younger men through HemisFair Park in San Antonio, Texas, about 10:30 at night. I thought this to be a strange event. I waved hello, not wanting to impose, but Robert Bly called to me, "Have you seen your father lately?" I had not. "Go find your father," he said, and walked on. His injunction represents, as you likely know, one of Robert's missions. It began, for me, an examination of faith.

Examinations of faith infuse nearly every line of this 2014 edition of *New Letters*. Imagine the boys in Rashaan Alexis Meneses' story "The Others Are Strangers," going to meet their father for dinner in another town. Imagine their deepest, yet unstated question, *In whom can we have faith?* Callum and, to a degree, his brother Ewan, want to know if their father is that person. Literature tends to expose the spiritual longings of its characters and, as such, allows us a look at ourselves. Somewhere, deep in the non-canonical Gospel of Thomas, we read, in Willis Barnstone's translation, "If you reveal what is within you, what you have will save you."

I am one, however, who needs help. I need examples, guides. Lao-tzu says in the *Tao Te Ching*, translated by Stephen Mitchell, "I have just three things to teach: simplicity, patience, compassion." Yes, I need all of those. "There's only one rule I know of, babies," proclaims Vonnegut's Mr. Rosewater at the hospital nursery, "You've got to be kind." At my father's funeral recently, I shook the hand of person after person my father had, one way or another, saved. That's the word they used, saved — he found them jobs, repaired their plumbing, drove them to the hospital, paid for and delivered groceries. He was my guide. I choose to be a celebrant.

"There is light within a person of light," Thomas adds. Poet Linda Pastan, in a poem on the centennial of the birth of William Stafford, proclaims her faith in him, a spiritual father. "How complicated such simplicities are," she writes, suggesting the need for Stafford's own examples of patience and compassion. Faith can be fragile.

The Vedanta philosophy says that our expectations are our greatest source of suffering. I once overheard the poet Lucille Clifton counsel an adolescent girl, suffering from some failure she saw in her mother. "You must have been born believing that your parents have to be perfect," Clifton said. To be in heaven, the Vedanta say, is to realize God in our own consciousness. Define God for yourself, of course, but literature helps us by exposing consciousness in others, by allowing us to participate in the moral complications of those outside of ourselves.

Recently, in Seattle, I had the joy of meeting for the first time the writer Brian Doyle. Our conversation drifted to the virtues of Oregon wines, especially the pinot noirs; but, as we talked, I thought mostly of how the character of his stories and essays have lifted my spirit over the years. He often writes of religious people, as in his story "The Archbishop Loses His Faith," but not for the religion, for the people. They struggle among the complicated simplicities; they err, sometimes badly, and seek to regain not only their faith but the state of being in which others can have faith in them.

In an interview I conducted in 2013 with poet Janice N. Harrington, she discusses faith in the person of her mother. I say *the person of* because her mother is a *person* first, complicated and worthy. We must get that. Literature shows us how to look beyond the complications to the essential perfection of our best selves. That is what we try to do here, as art tries to do, not only to have faith but to offer faith.

Notes

Essays written for the following editions of *New Letters*:

"Heroes" for vol. 71 no. 2, 2005.
"Resilience" for vol. 78 nos. 3 & 4, 2012.
"The Narrow Gate" for vol. 76 no. 1, 2009.
"On Wishful Thinking" for vol. 72 nos. 3 & 4, 2006.
"Typhoon" for vol. 71 no. 4, 2005.
"Glory" for vol. 69 no. 4, 2003.
"Form" for vol. 72 no. 1, 2005.
"All That I Remember" for vol. 72 no. 2, 2006.
"Art and Work" (as "Slope Failure") for vol. 73 no. 4, 2007.
"Fast and Slow" for vol. 77 no. 1, 2010.
"Service" for vol. 73 no. 2, 2007.
"Time and the Fabric of Immensity" for vol. 74 no. 3, 2008.
"Literary Values" for vol. 71 no. 1, 2004.
"Take This Seriously" for vol. 74 no. 4, 2008.
"Power" for vol. 77 no. 2, 2011.
"Madness" for vol. 70 nos. 3 & 4, 2004.
"Cry of the Renegade" for vol. 78 no. 1, 2011.
"The Goldilocks Zone" for vol. 80 no. 1, 2013.
"Faith" (as "Such Simplicity") for vol. 80 no. 2, 2014.

List of Poems Included

"Nurse's Epitaph," by Mia Leonin
"The Lord Is Easy to Please," by Allison Eir Jenks
"Woodbridge," by Mary Crockett Hill
"I'm Not Sure the Cherry Tree is the 'Loveliest of Trees,'" by
    Wendy Barker
"To My Poem of Hope," by Marilyn Kallet

Acknowledgments

With gratitude, I acknowledge the support of my coworkers at *New Letters* magazine, *New Letters on the Air*, and BkMk Press, especially since I moved from being managing editor to editor in 2002. Their contributions to our work here have been inspiring and essential. I am especially indebted to Ben Furnish at BkMk Press, whom I often ask to review my editor's essays in draft form. In more ways than I can list, our publications and broadcasts have thrived due entirely to the dedication of Betsy Beasley, Angela Elam, Ben, Stephanie Hughes, Ashley Kaine, Susan Schurman, and Jamie Walsh. I would also cite the assistance of Blaire Ginsburg, for her proofreading help, and recognize the good work of former staff members Dennis Conrow, Aleatha Ezra, Amy Lucas, and the many interns and volunteers we continue to welcome.

A profound thanks, also, for the guidance of my predecessors and bosses David Ray and James McKinley. Most important, I am given heart every day by the unfailing encouragement and intelligence of my wife, Lisa Dawes Stewart.

About the Author

Robert Stewart is editor of *New Letters* magazine, *New Letters on the Air*, a nationally syndicated literary radio program, and BkMk Press at the University of Missouri-Kansas City, where he also teaches poetry writing, magazine writing, and magazine editing. He has won a National Magazine Award for Editorial Achievement in the Essay category, from the American Society of Magazine Editors. His books include *Outside Language: Essays* (Helicon Nine Editions, a finalist in the PEN Center USA Literary Awards; and winner of the Thorpe Menn Award), *Plumbers* (poems, BkMk Press), and others. Poems have appeared in *Denver Quarterly, The Iowa Review, Poetry Northwest, Prairie Schooner, Mangrove, Stand, Notre Dame Review, The Literary Review* and other magazines. Anthology editorships include *Spud Songs: An Anthology of Potato Poems* (with Gloria Vando, benefit for hunger relief), and *Decade: Modern American Poets* (with Trish Reeves) and *Voices From the Interior*. He also is co-editor of the collection *New American Essays* (with Conger Beasley Jr., *New Letters*/BkMk Press).

www.ingramcontent.com/pod-product-compliance
Lightning Source LLC
Chambersburg PA
CBHW020018050426
42450CB00005B/540